Praying with

Sacred Beads

Praying with

Sacred

Beads

JOAN HUTSON

LIGUORI/TRIUMPH
LIGUORI, MISSOURI

Written to help you
help your hands
to help the prayer
in your heart to
be all it can be.

Published by Liguori/Triumph
An Imprint of Liguori Publications
Liguori, Missouri
www.liguori.org

Copyright 2000 by Joan Hutson

Library of Congress Cataloging-in-Publication Data

Hutson, Joan.
        Praying with sacred beads / Joan Hutson.
            p. cm.
        ISBN 0-7648-0569-X (hardcover)
        1. Rosary. I. Title.

BX2310.R7 H88 2000
242'.7 21; aa05 11-18—dc99   99-057763

Printed in the United States of America
04 03 02 01 00   5 4 3 2 1
First Edition

Contents

The History of
Prayer Beads

There is evidence that prayer beads were in use back in the third century. Today they are used in most of the world's major religions.

In the early Christian traditions, the desert Fathers carried a set number of pebbles which they discarded one at a time as the prescribed prayers were said. This practice evolved into a cord with a set number of pebbles or beads on it. This began the evolution of the Christian rosary in both Eastern and Western Christianity.

The Eastern and Western Churches had a great devotion to the Psalter of David—the Book of Psalms. They divided the psalms into three parts of fifty psalms each. The "three fifties" were recited by lay people as well as monastics. There were prescribed numbers of times that the Psalter was to be recited for those who had died. To accommodate monks and lay people who could not read, little psalters were composed based on the repetition of the Lord's Prayer and the Angelical Salutation 150 times, divided into three fifties which compares to the Catholic rosary of today. The

Western rosary was used as a substitute for the Psalter.

Monks in the desert developed intense prayer lives where they repeated short prayers throughout the day to develop the prayer of the heart. One of those prayers has been carried up to the present, known today as the Jesus Prayer. It is: "Jesus, Son of the Living God, have mercy on me." Prayer ropes consisting of 100 to 300 knots or beads were devised to help one keep track of the number of recitations.

Monks often recited the prayer up to 12,000 times each day until the prayer actually became self-active, continuing on in the heart unceasingly, day and night.

In addition to a prayer rope or "chotki" they used a leather counter with steps or ladders called the "vervitsa" or "step-ladder to heaven." Today monks and nuns of the East are given the chotki or vervitsa during their monastic profession. They wear them on their left hand as a reminder to pray always.

Muslims use prayer beads for counting with devotion the names and sacred attributes of

Allah, their god. Buddhists use prayer beads whose basic number is 108 which is said to represent the number of earthly desires which mortals have. A chanting ritual accompanies the use of the beads. Their rosary consists of two circles of beads that are interconnected with one another. Holding down one bead on one circle while going around the other allows one to keep count of over 35,000 prayers! The Eastern Church uses woolen rosaries with 33, 50, 100, 150, and 300 knots. The Celts rosary consists of 150 knots or beads to accommodate the recitation of the Psalter.

There are various forms of the rosary developing today that are quite removed from the classical rosary prayer. These are known as chaplets. The term is used to designate the beads themselves and the prayers used with them. They vary in theme as well as the number of beads involved. There is the "Cross Chaplet" which consists of 33 beads to correspond to the 33 years of Christ's life on earth. There are chaplets of the Immaculate Conception, Saint

Anthony, Saint Anne, Saint Thérèse, and Saint Patrick. There is a chaplet of the Trinitarian Creed based on the ancient creeds of the Church, particularly the Nicene Creed and the Apostles' Creed.

In the chaplet of Saint Michael the Archangel the nine choirs of angels are honored. The history of this chaplet is based on a vision where Saint Michael promised that anyone who would practice this devotion would have an escort of nine angels chosen from the nine choirs when approaching holy Communion.

The chaplet of "the Divine Mercy" is perhaps the most popular of all chaplets today. It is sung daily by thousands over national television. Recited or sung on ordinary rosary beads it has its own special ritual of repeated prayers.

The use of prayer beads aids contemplative prayer by bringing into use the body, the mind, and the spirit. The feel of the bead in the fingers helps to keep the mind from wandering while the ordered rhythm of the prayers leads one into stillness. Sacred beads are used to slow down the mind to a new level of consciousness where we reclaim our relationship with Spirit.

The prayers in this collection are based on ten beads. The form of the beads could be as simple as ten knots tied in a cord.

PART ONE

Knowing and Sanctifying Me

Preparatory PRAYER

Inhale with a double breath breathing in Light.

Exhale with a double breath breathing out darkness.

MEDITATION ON
God's Presence

Pray: In the stillness of my soul

O my God,

I am aware of Your sacred Presence

As I remain in Your radiation of Love

I ask that You:

purify me (bead one)

forgive me (bead two)

enlighten me (bead three)

inspire me (bead four)

teach me (bead five)

lead me (bead six)

use me (bead seven)

empower me (bead eight)

transform me (bead nine)

indwell me (bead ten)

MEDITATION OF
Self-Evaluation

Pray: O God, help me to see the faults in me

    that tend to make me

    stop loving myself.

    I will study these traits in me:

        pride (bead one)

        jealousy (bead two)

        anger (bead three)

        unforgivingness (bead four)

        spiritual sloth (bead five)

            idolatry (bead six)

            lust (bead six)

            gluttony (bead seven)

            excess materialism (bead eight)

            lovelessness (bead nine)

            Godlessness (bead ten)

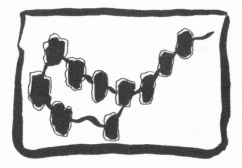

MEDITATION ON
Knowing Thyself

Pray: In an attempt to understand me,

    O Lord,

anoint my inner wisdom

in this appraisal of myself.

This is what I accept about myself:

    (one attribute pondered on each bead)

This is what I do not accept about myself:

    (one attribute pondered on each bead)

MEDITATION ON
Visualization

Pray: O Everlasting Father,

I visualize myself in the following roles.

I see myself and observe my thoughts,

words, and actions

in these roles of:

a joyful person (bead one)

a compassionate person (bead two)

a generous person (bead three)

a respected person (bead four)

a truthful person (bead five)

a patient person (bead six)

a faith-filled person (bead seven)

a thankful person (bead eight)

a loving person (bead nine)

a holy person (bead ten)

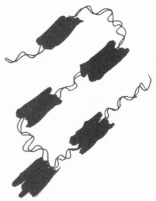

MEDITATION ON
Ego Awareness

Pray: Lord, keep me ever aware

　　　that it is my ego

　　who delights in keeping me

　　　feeling separate—

　　superior and inferior.

　　　And alone.

　　Help me determine

　　　in every thought, word, or deed

　　whether I am serving ego or You

　　in the following:

in my prayers	(bead one)
in my charity	(bead two)
in my conversations	(bead three)
in my judgments	(bead four)
in my community actions	(bead five)
in my liturgical actions	(bead six)
in my relationships	(bead seven)
in my meditations	(bead eight)
in my correspondence	(bead nine)
in my love for You	(bead ten)

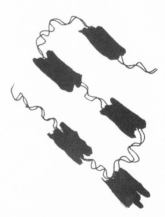

MEDITATION ON
Forgiveness

Pray: O God,

    I willingly drop the overwhelming weight

      of remembered grievances.

    I forgive whoever comes to mind as I hold

      each prayer bead.

name   (bead one)

name   (bead two)

name   (bead three)

name   (bead four)

name   (bead five)

name   (bead six)

name   (bead seven)

name   (bead eight)

name   (bead nine)

name   (bead ten)

MEDITATION OF
Thanksgiving

Pray: Blessed are You,

Creator of the Universe,

who has given me:

(State what you have been given on each bead.)

thank you for... (bead one)

thank you for... (bead two)

thank you for... (bead three)

thank you for... (bead four)

thank you for... (bead five)

thank you for... (bead six)

thank you for... (bead seven)

thank you for... (bead eight)

thank you for... (bead nine)

thank you for... (bead ten)

MEDITATION ON
Understanding Illness

Pray: O Universal Healer,

remind me that illness is a manifestation

of the soul's pain and confusion and stress

manifesting physically so that

my consciousness

may recognize it.

I will meditate on possible areas

of aggravation:

an unforgiving spirit (bead one)

a dishonest spirit (bead two)

an envious spirit (bead three)

an angry spirit (bead four)

a critical spirit (bead five)

an immoral spirit (bead six)

an untruthful spirit (bead seven)

a greedy spirit (bead eight)

a cynical spirit (bead nine)

an abusive spirit (bead ten)

PRAYING *with* SACRED BEADS

PART TWO

Thankful Praise

Preparatory PRAYER

Inhale with a double breath breathing in love.
Exhale with a double breath breathing out love.

MEDITATION ON
God's Presence

Pray: In the stillness of my soul,

O my God,

I am aware of Your sacred Presence.

As I remain in Your radiation of Love

I praise you for your wonders of creation:

Your pastel ribbons of dawn
(bead one)

Your hillsides of wild flowers
opening to the morning sun
(bead two)

Your rain-rinsed morning
breezes (bead three)

Your blue ocean waves
smoothing white beach sands
(bead four)

Your autumn winds stripping
naked the willow trees
(bead five)

Your snowflakes one by one
filling up the woods (bead six)

Your world under a mantle
of white (bead seven)

Your spring winds unlocking the
frozen streams (bead eight)

Your dusk shadowing the day
sounds (bead nine)

Your stars splintering the night
sky (bead ten)

MEDITATION ON PRAISE FOR
Sacred Attributes

Pray: I praise You, Lord,

from all the altars of the world

for Your:

power that holds the universe on course (bead one)

power that sustains the heavenly choirs in unceasing song (bead two)

power that commands the many legions of angels (bead three)

power that overturns all forces of evil (bead four)

power that creates miracles when needed (bead five)

power that controls all forces of nature
(bead six)

power that converts nations
(bead seven)

power that enlightens worldwide
(bead eight)

power that transforms souls worldwide
(bead nine)

power with instant global reach
(bead ten)

MEDITATION OF
Praise for Humanity

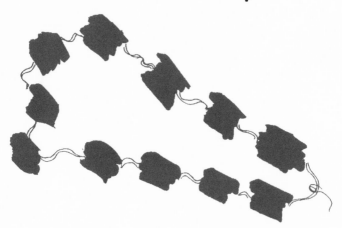

Pray: I praise You, Lord, for Your creation

of a caring humanity. I praise You

especially for:

the parents who gave me life (bead one)

those who nurtured and shaped me
through childhood (bead two)

those who helped me see and
materialize dreams (bead three)

those whose interaction helped me
to grow (bead four)

those who loved me too much to let
me grow wayward (bead five)

those who showed me the value
of suffering and sacrifice (bead six)

those who encouraged when hope
was almost gone (bead seven)

those whose own lives were heroic
examples of a life well lived (bead eight)

those who urged me on to the highest
heights possible (bead nine)

those whose holiness would never allow
me to stop reaching for You (bead ten)

MEDITATION OF
Thanksgiving

Pray: Lord, I thank You for everything
         in Your creation
that fits in Your rainbow of colors:

PRAYING *with* SACRED BEADS

for all I can think of that is red   (bead one)

for all I can think of that is orange   (bead two)

for all I can think of that is yellow   (bead three)

for all I can think of that is green   (bead four)

for all I can think of that is blue   (bead five)

for all I can think of that is violet   (bead six)

for all I can think of that is black   (bead seven)

for all I can think of that is white   (bead eight)

for all I can think of that is silver   (bead nine)

for all I can think of that is gold   (bead ten)

PART THREE

Visualization and Affirmation

Preparatory PRAYER

Inhale with a double breath breathing in
    empowering Light.
Exhale with a double breath breathing out
    disabling darkness.

MEDITATION ON
God's Presence

Pray: In the stillness of my soul,

O my God,

I am aware of Your sacred Presence.

As I remain in Your radiation of Love

I am empowered to say:

You love me (bead one)

I love me
(bead two)

You accept me fully (bead three)

I accept me fully (bead four)

You forgive all my mistakes (bead five)

I forgive all my mistakes (bead six)

I am wonderfully made in Your sight
(bead seven)

I am wonderfully made in my sight (bead eight)

I am precious in Your sight (bead nine)

I am precious in my sight
(bead ten)

Visualizing Virtues

Pray: I want to be pleasing in Your sight,

O Lord.

I see myself:

praying (bead one)

chanting praise (bead two)

lifting my hands in praise (bead three)

leading others in praise (bead four)

feeding the hungry (bead five)

sheltering the homeless (bead six)

visiting the sick (bead seven)

visiting the imprisoned (bead eight)

teaching the Gospels (bead nine)

spreading the Gospels
(bead ten)

AFFIRMATIONS
Discipline

Pray: O God, with Your grace
nothing is impossible.
Believing this, I can say
with conviction:

> I am in full control of my thoughts (bead one)
>
> I am in full control of my words (bead two)
>
> I am in full control of my actions (bead three)
>
> I am in full control of my appetites (bead four)
>
> I am in full control of my desires (bead five)
>
> I am in full control of my judgments (bead six)
>
> I am in full control of my decisions
> (bead seven)
>
> I am in full control of my responsibilities
> (bead eight)
>
> I am in full control of my service to others
> (bead nine)
>
> I am in full control of my service to God
> (bead ten)

PART FOUR

Intercession

Preparatory PRAYER

Inhale with a double breath breathing in
    unconditional love.
Exhale with a double breath breathing out
    unconditional love.

MEDITATION ON
God's Presence

Pray: In the stillness of my soul,

O my God,

I am aware of Your sacred Presence.

As I remain in Your radiation of Love

I ask that You rescue with Your Almighty power

those who at this moment:

are tempted to do serious wrong
(bead one)

are victims of abuse
(bead two)

are victims of addiction
(bead three)

are victims of intolerable physical pain
(bead four)

are victims of extreme poverty
(bead five)

are victims of a devastating relationship
(bead six)

are victims of unjust discrimination
(bead seven)

are victims of poor parenting
(bead eight)

are victims of violent behavior
(bead nine)

are victims of anger against You, God
(bead ten)

INTERCESSION OF
Blessing

Pray: O Lord,
I ask that You
bless with Your
deepest grace:

me	(bead one)
my family	(bead two)
my neighborhood	(bead three)
my city	(bead four)
my country	(bead five)
my state	(bead six)
my nation	(bead seven)
my continent	(bead eight)
my planet	(bead nine)
my universe	(bead ten)

 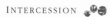

MEDITATION OF
Personal Blessing

Pray: O Lord,

You see into the depths

of all hearts,

bless the person who comes

to mind on each bead

with the grace You know they need:

name (bead one)

name (bead two)

name (bead three)

name (bead four)

name (bead five)

name (bead six)

name (bead seven)

name (bead eight)

name (bead nine)

name (bead ten)

PART FIVE

Praying the Psalms on Prayer Beads

Preparatory PRAYER

Inhale with a double breath breathing in the blessing
　　of the psalms.

Exhale with a double breath breathing out to all the
　　blessings of the psalms.

MEDITATION ON
God's Presence

Pray: O Lord,

　　　bless my meditations

　　　as I pray the quintessential message

　　　of each psalm

　　　as I revolve through

　　　my prayer beads.

PSALM 1
Blessed is the one
Who delights in God's law
That one will surely
Prosper in all things...

PSALM 2
All you rulers of the land
You must serve the God
You are trying in vain
To silence...

PSALM 3
I cry out to my God
Feeling His closeness to me
Holding me
In perfect peace...

PSALM 4
I have realized
More happiness in God
Than all the pleasures
The world can give...

PSALM 5
Morning after morning
I call
And God answers me
Clearing clouded skies…

PSALM 6
Wounded with heartbreak
Weeping throughout the long, long night
O my God
How long, how long…

PSALM 7
O my God
Justify me
Re-establish my honor
Acquit me, Lord…

PSALM 8
O my majestic God
How vast is your universe
And yet
You know me by name…

PSALM 9
You, I praise O Lord
Exalting You
Extolling You
Proclaiming You
Loving You…

PSALM 10
Defender of all creation
Lift up waning spirits
Wipe away tears
Heal all broken hearts…

PSALM 11
I must always be aware
That God is always aware
Of me
And all my needs…

PSALM 12
Lord, I trust Your Word
Always
As pure as refined silver
Always without compromise…

PSALM 13
Lord, how long, how long
Must my tears trail in sorrow
Still
Still trusting in You…

PSALM 14
God looks down to earth
Searching for one
Who is searching for Him
All are turned away…

PSALM 15
Who abides in God's heart
Those who heal rather than hurt
And those
Who love rather than hate…

PSALM 16
Apart from God
My life is a barren desert
But with Him
A blooming field.

PSALM 17

Someday in righteousness
I will see Your Face
O God
And be fully satisfied…

PSALM 18

Under threatening storm clouds
God pulled me from deep waters
To stand securely on the heights…

PSALM 19

The heavens proclaim
The handiwork of our God
Their jubilant voices
Everywhere….

PSALM 20

May God answer you
May He send you help from heaven
All you plan
Succeeding…

PSALM 21
All who trust in God
Will never be shaken and tossed
Thrown about
By chaotic winds...

PSALM 22
All the earth proclaims
And bows in reverence
Before the Lord
Fragrant incense rising...

PSALM 23
The Lord is my Shepherd
There is nothing I shall want
He leads me to quiet waters
And I fear nothing...

PSALM 24
The earth belongs to God
His are the mountains and the hills,
His are the rivers and streams
His, the Universe...

PSALM 25

All who hope in God
Will never be put to shame
Weighted in darkness
Or shadowed in doubt.

PSALM 26

O God, how I love Your House
The shrine of Your glory
The home of Your brilliance
Your Presence dwelling...

PSALM 27

The Lord is my Light
He leads me
Down clear paths
Paths lit by His grace...

PSALM 28

The Lord is my strength
If He does not answer my cries
There is no one else
No one...

PSALM 29
The voice of the Lord
Thunders, resounds
Shakes, breaks
Unveiling awesome power…

PSALM 30
Weeping through the night
The long, long night
But with the morning sun comes joy
To dance through the day…

PSALM 31
Though I am confused by anguish
Broken in health
Steeped in sadness
I trust in You, O God…

PSALM 32
Admitting my sin
Confessing my guilt
Expressing my sorrow
I again feel joy…

PSALM 33
God who made our hearts
God who watches over them
Extends
His protective Hand...

PSALM 34
All brokenhearted ones
God is very close to you
Aware
Of every tear...

PSALM 35
O God,
Speak up for me
Stop those plotting my downfall
You are my only hope...

PSALM 36
O God
Do not allow
The arrogance of sinners
To influence me
To turn from You...

PSALM 37
Never envy those
Who seem to thrive by evil
To win by wrong
For justice will prevail…

PSALM 38
O God,
My heart beats wildly
My body reflects my pain
All woundings are open…

PSALM 39
Truly life is but a breath
My stay on this earth
Very brief
A mere moment to God…

PSALM 40
God drew me up
Lifted me out of the mire and mud
Standing me on Rock
Free…

PSALM 41
So precious in God's eyes
Are those who give of themselves
Not counting cost
To help the troubled…

PSALM 42
Deep calls unto deep
And in the mighty roar of the waterfall
It is God's song
That is eternally singing…

PSALM 43
May Your penetrating Light and Truth
Break into my deep darkness
Turning
My night into dawn…

PSALM 44
Lord, I desperately need Your help
And I can't seem to reach You
O God,
Will You reach for me…

PSALM 45

O let inspiring thought arise
Let my heart speak eloquently
Verses
For my God and King...

PSALM 46

Yes, I have no fear at all
Though the earth gives way
And the mountains twist and surge
For God is my Security...

PSALM 47

God is forever our God
He is not to be rationalized
Out of existence
He is everlasting...

PSALM 48

How great is our God
Soaring high above our wisdom
Transcending
Human thought.

PSALM 49
Be not among those
Who think
They do not need God
The only One who can save...

PSALM 50
Give to God a celebration
A banquet of highest praise
Love and thankfulness
Flowing...

PSALM 51
Lord, may Your mercy
Leave not a trace of memory
To now or ever
Condemn me...

PSALM 52
Like a flourishing olive tree
I thrive in the house of the Lord
Vibrant
And growing, growing...

PSALM 53
God looks down from above
Looking for one who does good
Searching, searching
Is there even one…

PSALM 54
O God,
Save me by Your might
Sustain me
Sustain me by Love…

PSALM 55
O, to fly away
To fly away with the wings of a white dove
Through clouded skies
Into far off peace…

PSALM 56
O God,
You have seen my many tears
You have seen my restless nights
You have seen that I am still trusting…

PSALM 57
Be exalted, O my God
Be exalted over all the earth
Your glory rising
My praises soaring…

PSALM 58
Yes, we have a God
A just God
A God who has the last word
In judging the earth…

PSALM 59
O rescue me, my God
From the enemies of my soul
Turn them away
Fracture their deceitful plans…

PSALM 60
We are desperate, O Lord
Mend the earth's fractures and deep pain
Arise
And raise Your Victory…

PSALM 61
O Lord,
Hear my cry
And listen to the longing of my heart
Quiet the throbbings
Quiet the tremblings…

PSALM 62
My heart waits
My heart waits for God
All I need comes from Him
All I want comes from Him…

PSALM 63
O God
From a parched land
I cry to You
Thirsting for Living Water…

PSALM 64
From conspiracy upon conspiracy
From arrows aimed at my heart
Shield me
O saving God…

PSALM 65
God cares for His land
For His valleys waving with grain
For His hills mantled in gladness
For his rivers laughing and clear...

PSALM 66
God tests and tries us
In the crucible of life
Purifying
And transforming...

PSALM 67
All the nations of the earth
Who allow God to be their God
Will prosper
Will prosper with joy...

PSALM 68
All you singers
All you musicians
Let your music bless the land
With holy love songs...

PSALM 69
Save me,
Save me, O God,
Deep waters swiftly rise
Deep torrents of fear threaten…

PSALM 70
Lord,
Hasten to help me
Come quickly to aid me
Quickly, Lord, quickly…

PSALM 71
Lord,
You have been my hope
My confidence since birth
You are never far away…

PSALM 72
God rules from sea to sea
Outlasting sun and moon
Mountains and sea
Ever reigning with justice…

PSALM 73
My heart was grieved
I envied evildoers
But through my embitterment
I learned how hollow were their victories...

PSALM 74
O God,
There is so little left
To show we are Your people
Restore Your image, O Lord
Restore Your image...

PSALM 75
God judges rightly
He humbles one
He exalts another
All in appointed time...

PSALM 76
God desires peace
Breaking all weapons of war
Asking earth
To fall on its knees...

PSALM 77
O God,
I struggle through sleepless nights
Reaching in vain for solace
Am I forgotten…

PSALM 78
O listen to God's teachings
Truths we have heard from of old
Unchanging truth
Word telling word…

PSALM 79
Evildoers scoff
They seem to greatly prosper
How long, Lord,
How long…

PSALM 80
O God,
Watch over this vine
This root that Your Hand has planted
As it yields its fruit…

PSALM 81

God gives times of great joy
And times of great trial
Scheduling them into our days
For the complete celebration of life...

PSALM 82

O God,
Rescue the weak
For they walk about in darkness
Not knowing
They are heirs of Your kingdom...

PSALM 83

O Lord,
Be not silent
For Your enemies are astir
Creating havoc...

PSALM 84

O how happy are they
Who worship in God's temple
How rich the praise
How holy the praise...

PSALM 85
O Lord,
We are sorely misled
By God-less philosophies
O turn us back to You…

PSALM 86
One in mind and heart
Undivided in my love
Undivided in my allegiance
I live trusting in You…

PSALM 87
Those who scorn God
Cannot live in His Holy City
Instead
They roam the wastelands…

PSALM 88
Day and night I cry
Sadness is my only friend
There is no light in my darkness
My unending darkness…

PSALM 89
With overflowing heart
I will sing of God's goodness
Forever I will sing
My song will know no end...

PSALM 90
Before the dawn sky
Before the earth was brought forth from nothingness
You were
O great God...

PSALM 91
Remember
When God is your God
The terror of threatening night
Will never be yours...

PSALM 92
O Lord
I proclaim Your Name
At the break and close of day
As an unending lyric...

PSALM 93
Our God is King
The ocean breakers thundering His praise
From shore to shore
Without ceasing...

PSALM 94
O God of justice
O God to whom vengeance belongs
Right the wrongs we see
All around us...

PSALM 95
O people
Bow down in worship
Kneel before the Lord your God
O hear Him calling...

PSALM 96
O earth listen
O earth rejoice
Honor the nearness of God
In His creation...

PSALM 97

Sing out, you mainlands
Sing praise, you islands afar
Distant shores, exult
Creation, praise…

PSALM 98

Let the oceans clap their waves
Let the hills sing forth their praises
All creation
Announcing the goodness of God…

PSALM 99

Give God reverence
Perceive His most holy splendor
Hold your breath in awe
In holy atmosphere…

PSALM 100

O people
Let all see your joy
As your praise enters His courts
And then returns
To bless you…

PSALM 101
O Lord
I do want to walk down
The path of rightful living
Though that path be narrow...

PSALM 102
Yes,
God's renown lives on
Lasting through generation after generation
An unbroken message...

PSALM 103
I know
God forgives my sins
Wiping them completely away
Remembering no more...

PSALM 104
Universal God
Through your wisdom
The sun knows its position
The stars, their places...

PSALM 105
Sing,
Sing the Lord songs
That translate His miracles
Into love lyrics...

PSALM 106
O how patient is God
Pursuing me with His care
And
Following me with His love...

PSALM 107
All set free by God
Tell of the wonderful joy
That is now theirs
Beyond expectation...

PSALM 108
Awake, O harp and lyre
Awaken the dawn with me
With ecstatic song
And ecstatic heart...

PSALM 109
O God
Be not still
When I receive evil for good
And hatred for love...

PSALM 110
I will be renewed
From the womb of the new dawn
Forever
The Lord at my side...

PSALM 111
Great
O great are all God's works
Too great to ever be forgotten
Instilling wonder...
Instilling reverence...

PSALM 112
For the generous loving heart
Light shines even in darkness
Fear is unknown
Unknown...

PRAYING *with* SACRED BEADS

PSALM 113
Who
Who is like our God
Exalted over nations
Enthroned in Light…

PSALM 114
Tremble now
Tremble now, O earth
You are in God's true Presence
And you can expect miracles…

PSALM 115
O Lord,
Not to us, not to us
But to Your Name be glory
Now and forever…

PSALM 116
O my soul
Be at rest
The Lord has been good to you
In your needs, He comes…

PSALM 117
All you nations
Praise the Lord
Extol Him, everyone
He loves us all...

PSALM 118
Give thanks
Give thanks to the Lord
His love endures forever
To time beyond all time...

PSALM 119
Lord,
Open my eyes
To see the truth in Your Word
By day and by night...

PSALM 120
O my God
Teach me
How to be a peacemaker
In a hostile world...

PSALM 121
My help comes from God
Who watches
Never slumbers
My ever wakeful God…

PSALM 122
O yes,
My heart leaped for joy
When anyone suggested
We go to God's house…

PSALM 123
Watching
Watching and waiting
My eyes upon You, my Lord
Anticipating…

PSALM 124
Know
Were God not with us
Rage would have swept us away
In torrents of hate...

PSALM 125
The Lord surrounds me
Surrounds me
Like a massive rock mountain
Total protection...

PSALM 126
Those who sow in tears
Carrying seed to be sown
Will return
Singing...

PRAYING *with* SACRED BEADS

PSALM 127

Unless the Lord builds
Builders labor in vain
For only what the Lord approves
Will last...

PSALM 128

Blest,
Blest are you who love God
Prosperity will be yours
There will be joy around your table...

PSALM 129

Yes,
I have been oppressed
Much oppressed from my youth
But never overcome...

PSALM 130

If You keep in mind
O Lord
Our sins
Who of us would survive...

PSALM 131
I have stilled my soul
I am quiet before You
My God
My askings now stilled...

PSALM 132
O God,
I will not sleep
Until I find a place for You
A worshiping space within...

PSALM 133
O how pleasant
How pleasant it is
When all live in harmony
Blest symphony...

PSALM 134
Lift up your praising hands
Exalt with your praising voice
Love with your praising heart
The Lord your God...

PSALM 135
Idols of the world
Have speechless mouths
Have sighted eyes
Our God speaks, sees, loves...

PSALM 136
Everyone
Give thanks to God
For the earth beneath our feet
For the skies above...

PSALM 137
O Lord
How can we sing songs
Of joy
In a captive state...

PSALM 138
God
I called and You answered
You never abandoned me
I who am the work of Your Hands...

PSALM 139
I am wonderfully made
And completely known by You, O God
Ever in Your Mind
Always in Your Heart...

PSALM 140
O Lord
You are my God
Rescue me from violence
Shatter evil schemes...

PSALM 141
O Lord
Guard my mouth
Keep watch over my heart
Lest evil traps me...

PSALM 142
O saving God
Free me,
Ransom me from the prison
I have built myself...

PSALM 143
O God
Come quickly
My depression deepens
My life is without design...

PSALM 144
I know
I am but a mere breath
A thin wisp of morning wind
Why do You care so for me...

PSALM 145
All eyes look to You
My God
You satisfy the desire
Of every living thing...

PSALM 146
Do not rely on the world
It has no power to save
Only God
Has the power to save you...

PSALM 147
How great is our God
How great is His goodness
His Word runs swiftly
Throughout the vast universe…

PSALM 148
O sun, moon, and shining stars
O wind, clouds, rain, and creation, all
Praise the Lord
Praise the Creator of it all…

PSALM 149
Sing,
Sing with all your heart
The high praises of your God
In a triumphant hymn of praise…

PSALM 150
Praise
Let us all sing praise
Instruments join the song
FOR OUR GOD IS GREAT…

PART SIX

Praying Words of Jesus

Preparatory PRAYER

Inhale with a double breath breathing in the Spirit of
Jesus.
Exhale with a double breath breathing out the Spirit
of Jesus.

MEDITATION ON
God's Presence

Pray: In the stillness of my soul

O my God,

I am aware of the Presence of Jesus.

As I remain in His radiation of Love

I meditate on His Words:

Come to Me…and find rest for your soul (bead one)

I am the Vine, you are the branch (bead two)

I am the Good Shepherd. I know mine, and mine
know Me (bead three)

I am the Bread of Life (bead four)

Love your enemies. Do good to those who hurt you
(bead five)

Forgive one another, as I have forgiven you (bead six)

Do unto others what you would want them to do
unto you (bead seven)

Do not judge or you, too, will be judged (bead eight)

Where your treasure is, there will your heart be
(bead nine)

Behold, I am with you always (bead ten)

INTENSE LITANIES ON
the Words of Jesus

Pray: Lord, I choose the words of Jesus that best fit

the sentiments of my heart at this moment

repeating the selection on all ten beads:

Seek first the Kingdom...

Come, all ye burdened...

Ask, and you will receive...

I am the way and the truth and the life...

Love one another...

If I set you free you will be free indeed...

He who is not with Me is against Me...

Peace, I give...

PRAYING
the Name of Jesus

Pray: I lift my heart in praise as I
meditate on these names of
Jesus:

Beloved Son of the Father	(bead one)
King of kings	(bead two)
Counselor	(bead three)
Savior	(bead four)
Highly exalted	(bead five)
Name above all names	(bead six)
Majestic Lord	(bead seven)
Almighty Lord	(bead eight)
Everlasting Love	(bead nine)
Prince of peace	(bead ten)

PRAYING
the Characteristics of Jesus

Pray: Jesus, Son of the Eternal Father,

Thank You for the following traits:

for ever present	(bead one)
for ever listening	(bead two)
for ever concerned	(bead three)
for ever understanding	(bead four)
for ever guiding	(bead five)

for ever forgiving	(bead six)
for ever inspiring	(bead seven)
for ever encouraging	(bead eight)
for ever protecting	(bead nine)
for ever loving	(bead ten)

INTERCESSORY PRAYER WITH
the Name of Jesus

Pray: You know the depths of the heart of the
person I am so concerned about. I link
Your Holy Name with the name of the
one I am praying for now....

Jesus, (name) on all ten beads.

MEDITATIONS ON
Scenes in the Life of Jesus

Pray: Jesus, I place myself in each of the following
scenes of Your life. I visualize how I would
have responded to You and to the environment
around You.

Your birth in Bethlehem (bead one)

Your childhood in Nazareth (bead two)

your baptism in the Jordan River (bead three)

Your temptations in the desert (bead four)

Your teaching on the hillsides (bead five)

Your healing of the multitudes (bead six)

Your Last Supper with Your apostles (bead seven)

Your agony in the garden (bead eight)

Your crucifixion (bead nine)

Your Resurrection (bead ten)

PART SEVEN

Singing Mantras of Prayer

Preparatory PRAYER

Inhale with a double breath mentally breathing in
    musical sound.
Exhale with a double breath mentally breathing out
    musical sound.

MEDITATION ON
God's Presence

Pray: In the stillness of my soul

O my God,

I am aware of Your sacred Presence

As I remain in Your radiation of Love

I sing as many revolutions

of my prayer beads

as the Spirit prompts,

using the familiar eighteenth-century melody

that is given,

or one I am inspired to compose,

or I take fragments of the prayers suggested

forming my own shorter prayers.

Presence

I come into Your Presence, I come into Your Presence,

I come into Your Presence, Your Holy Peace.

My soul is stilled and silent, my soul is stilled and silent, my soul is stilled and silent, in Love's Pure Light.

My heart now beats with Thine, Lord, My heart now beats with Thine, Lord, My heart now beats with Thine, Lord, in Love's accord.

Your peace is flowing through me, Your peace is flowing through me, Your peace is flowing through me, in waves of grace.

Your joy is coursing through me, Your joy is coursing through me, Your joy is coursing through me, in torrents deep.

I'm lost in awe and wonder, I'm lost in awe and wonder, I'm lost in awe and wonder, transcending thought.

Praise

I praise You for Your greatness, I praise You for Your greatness,

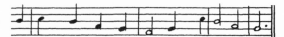

I praise You for You greatness, Majestic Lord.

I praise You for Creation, I praise You for Creation,
I praise You for Creation, Creator God.

I praise You for Your day skies, I praise You for Your day skies,
I praise You for Your day skies, ablaze with sun.

I praise You for Your day sounds, I praise You for Your day sounds,
I praise You for Your day sounds, of wind through leaves.

I praise You for Your night skies, I praise You for Your night skies,
I praise You for Your night skies, of soft moonlight.

I praise You for Your night sounds, I praise You for Your night
sounds, I praise You for Your night sounds, of silent stars.

I praise You for Your angels, I praise You for Your angels,
I praise You for Your angels, who protect me.

I praise You for the Glory, I praise You for the Glory,
I praise You for the Glory, You promise me.

Contrition

I come before You now, Lord, I come before You now, Lord,

I come before You now, Lord, with contrite heart.

I confess my faults, Lord, I confess my faults, Lord,
I confess my faults, Lord, with sorrow deep.

I know You do forgive me, I know You do forgive me,
I know You do forgive me, O caring God.

Now I forgive myself, Lord, now I forgive myself, Lord,
now I forgive myself, Lord, as You would want.

Adoration

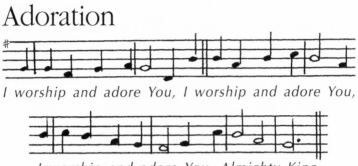

I worship and adore You, I worship and adore You,

I worship and adore You, Almighty King.

How glorious is Your Name, Lord, how glorious is Your Name, Lord, how glorious is Your Name, Lord, Majestic One.

Eternal is Your reign, Lord, eternal is Your reign, Lord, eternal is Your reign, Lord, and filled with care.

Your love is everlasting, Your love is everlasting, Your love is everlasting, O love divine.

I bow down before You, I bow down before You, I bow down before You, my Lord and God.

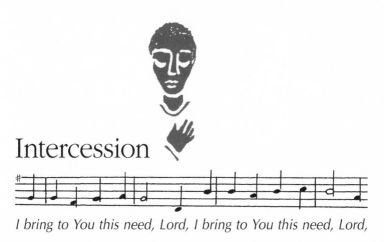

Intercession

I bring to You this need, Lord, I bring to You this need, Lord,

I bring to You this need, Lord, into Your hands.

I bring to You (name), Lord, I bring to You (name), Lord,
I bring to You (name), Lord, into Your hands.

I bring to You my family, I bring to You my family,
I bring to You my family, into Your hands.

I bring to You the world, Lord, I bring to You the world, Lord,
I bring to You the world, Lord, into Your hands.

I bring to You my Church, Lord, I bring to You my Church, Lord,
I bring to You my Church, Lord, into Your hands.

O may Your will be done, Lord, O may Your will be done, Lord,
O may your will be done, Lord, Your Holy Will.

Thanksgiving

I thank You for my life, Lord, I thank You for my life, Lord,

I thank You for my life, Lord, Your gift to me.

I thank you for my work, Lord, I thank You for my work, Lord, I thank You for my work, Lord, my way to serve.

I thank You for my sufferings, I thank You for my sufferings, I thank You for my sufferings, through them I grow.

I thank You for my joys, Lord, I thank You for my joys, Lord, I thank You for my joys, Lord, through them I praise.

Affirmations

I know I am enough, Lord, I know I am enough, Lord,

I know I am enough, Lord, for You made me.

I know I have enough, Lord, I know I have enough, Lord,
I know I have enough, Lord, for I have You.

I know I must diminish, I know I must diminish,
I know I must diminish, and You increase.

PART EIGHT

Mystical Prayer
on Prayer Beads

Preparatory PRAYER

Inhale with a double breath breathing in God.
Exhale with a double breath breathing out God.

MEDITATION ON
God's Presence

Pray: In the stillness of my soul

O my God

I am aware of Your sacred Presence.

As I remain in Your radiation of Love

I select a prayer word, FATHER,

which I return to whenever I

become aware that I am no

longer centered on Your Presence.

For every distraction that interrupts

my continued awareness of You,

I repeat my prayer word and

return to You. For twenty

minutes I will remain on

the first prayer bead

centered on You, O God.

Then I pray:

Our Father (bead two)
Who art in heaven (bead three)
Hallowed be Thy Name (bead four)
Thy kingdom come, thy will be done
on earth as it is in heaven. (bead five)
Give us this day our daily bread (bead six)
And forgive us our trespasses as we
forgive those who trespass against us (bead seven)
And lead us not into temptation
but deliver us from evil (bead eight)
For thine is the kingdom and the power
and the glory forever and ever (bead nine)
Amen. (bead ten)

PART NINE

Dwelling on the
Fruits of the
Holy Spirit

Preparatory PRAYER

Inhale with a double breath the Spirit of God.
Exhale with a double breath the Spirit of God.

MEDITATION ON
God's Presence

Pray: In the stillness of my soul

O my God,

I am aware of Your sacred Presence

As I remain in Your radiation of Love

I internalize these gifts of the Spirit

and dwell on one gift for as many

revolutions of my prayer beads as

the Spirit inspires.

Love

joy

peace

patience

kindness

goodness

faithfulness

gentleness

self-control

A Parting Word

Repetitio mater studiorum...that is, "Repetition is the mother of learning." It is also the channel into the deeper realms of the soul. As these prayers are repeated and sacredly moved through the fingers, may they also ignite the embers of contemplation and mystical union. That is my prayer for you...